ANALECTS

ON A CHINESE SCREEN

T0308993

ANALECTS

ON A CHINESE SCREEN

Glenn Mott

Chax Press

2 0 0 7

Cover photograph: Yijun Ge, *Chai* near Suzhou Creek, Shanghai, 2006

Library of Congress Cataloging-in-Publication Data

Mott, Glenn
   Analects on a Chinese screen / Glenn Mott.
      p. cm.
   ISBN 978-0-925904-61-4 (pbk. : alk. paper)
   1. China—Poetry. I. Title.

   PS3613.O844A53 2007
   811'.6—dc22

                              2006037248

Chax Press is supported by the Tucson Pima Arts Council and by the Arizona
Commission on the Arts with funding from the State of Arizona and the National
Endowment for the Arts.

Chax Press
101 W. 6th St.
Tucson, AZ 85701-1000
http://chax.org

Grateful acknowledgment is made to the editors of those journals who first printed
some of this work: *Delmar*, *New Orleans Review*, and *Tinfish*.

To the memory of Nick & Thelma Debenito,
my grandparents,
and their great good tavern.

And for D.A.—loyal opposition.

THE HERMITAGE OF AWARENESS

Not the unsayable
said.
        But the refusal to say
the unsaid.

        ●

The point where
the things
        one needs to say
are
    stronger than the need
to say them.

        ●

To be
      is explanation.

•

Near the window the air is good
                              with a view of the street.

Across the bar, wearing Marlboro gear, *liumang* pass out cigarettes like currency
         to their business associates.
                            A drinking contest ensues. They raise every glass
to a commanding: *Ganbei!*
                        In a little while, to the delight of all at the table,
one will show a day pack full of bundled $100 dollar bills.

•

I skim the mid-April inventory of construction disasters in a Shanghai daily
as I wait for a painter of Mickey Maoists,

                                        best known for the single iconic design he
repeats *ad nauseam.*

His products are regarded as those of a wayward invalid who has no general authority. But
this isn't the only reason to like him. He does not fear the monolith of representation.

He does not go out of himself to meet me in conversation, and works at painting as a
laborer from the provinces totes a cane balance of bricks.

He hasn't shown in New York at this point, but many of his designs have found their way
onto streetwear in San Francisco.

I am introduced to a woman named Tian Tian,
who smiles out at me, tonguing her gingiva as she does.

"There is no hope of failure in America," he tells me. Though I cannot tell if he decides
what this means, as I myself *es Americano,* & have hoped for as much as anyone.

"How is it possible so many people can have nothing foreign to say? That nothing is
foreign to her, yet she lives in isolation? America IS success," he says.

                                        It is not entirely convincing
to say I am a failure
here on the bounding main.

Nor can I recall the name Ed Ruscha
in time to answer his thoughts on lineage or influence.

•

Like DREAM in the American language,

                        SOUL in Chinese is inescapable.

•

Here's to lost Lutheran years, the hair shirt I never wore, the closeted self I liberated too soon, the indignation I never got to show, the contrivances of a searched soul.

If anything I'd say I know far too much of the interior to be of use to me.

Here are the sentences that I promised you. Which you may keep if you will regard & use them as the disconnected fragments of a completer essay.

To consider diminished expectations,
                              very soon, ambition appeased without joy or Double Happiness leaves for a success elsewhere.

Where there is hope for a new failure
of knowing motives.

•

Here a finger points.

           Something is finished in the margins. What a limited field made possible. Not by the main road, but found in a succession of fields trapped by roads and woods high in the bluffs. Your flint belongings in the creek beds,

                           a limited attraction is all the patron world has ever asked. Held within superstition now, the private collection of a Medici, perfection found in any school anthology.

But I can start here
with Byzantium.
           As students we asked often for an
explanation and were told of reeking artifice.

No one spoke of aging men.
Every fury on earth absorbed
                    in their priapic natures, no child
can understand.

•

There is something while reading *De Profundis*. In Oscar Wilde's descriptions of the events leading to his betrayal by Douglas.

That some of Douglas's more fucked-up characteristics fit me. And the realization then, that I wasn't self-identified with Wilde, but Douglas. The anatomy of that torn link with Wilde, the hero antagonist of his own diary. Repeating his betrayal, so that he might have something scandalous to read in his cell, that I might identify with the one who sent him up the river.

This is not to say that I knew the laws of my own being.

•

I'll tell you, much the most interesting thing about me
is that I am in China.
                    Sitting there with a notebook stashed in the pocket of a blue army
coat, smoking the mild Wuhu cigarettes of No. 1 Factory, Anhui Province.
                                                Kung says a
person wishing to establish his own character also establishes the character of another.

Kung instructs: *Go over the old so as to find out what is new.*
                                    Making the future
the oldest place of all.

Thinking of a use for himself one evening citizen Ah Qiu comes to a facing text: The life of
a young Chinese poet and his referent.

Have you thought cheerfully, I alone discovered the cargo cult of Walt Whitman, and saved
him from obscurity
                    in the library of Central High School.

Following the same precepts, Ah Qiu put lamp fires along the sides of Suzhou's misty
bridges and waited for the moon to show.

•

Though I lived in my car I was self-improving. I envied the patterned pencil's ragged edge.
I read *Uncle Tom's Cabin*.

I read Proust, but could not pronounce Sévigné, nor
could I finish *Swann's Way* in its wilted condition. On secluded trails high in the loess hills
with bottles of her mother's *vin de paille*, the color and smell of dried alfalfa hay, she
frequently appeased our troubles in the open air.

In the bee loud where the bumble suck'd
in the meadow's slip stunned and struck we lie, tracing slugs of contrail shot against the sky
on stratospheric zephyrs.

•

Do not mistake lines for poetry
                      like the white wine drunkard.

Give me this last chance at the words of my ineptitude.
To look and find what is unforeseen.

She is riding numb & trusting on a red August twilight, staring at the white line, radio
crisping with something we'd taken as I miss everything but the road in the headlights.

Charlie could have reached for Chan Parker as long as he wanted and still come up empty,
though she was good.

        There is a stubborn determination among the peoples of Northwest Missouri
not to be conned, and they realized, before I,
books would have no power to compensate the losses.

I came to the jackals of sensitivity with something like love,
the mind making too much of everything they were, with no appreciation
of modest and learned ignorance or anachronism
that would afflict the limits of their reason.

And Charlie begged Chan not to let them take him back to Kansas City,
at rest now, in Lincoln's Cemetery.

•

Thrill seeking
                    is not a Chinese characteristic. The words NEW and CURIOUS
applied to American things.

The common greeting *Chi fan le ma?*
                                        is a shibboleth of famine:
Have you eaten yet? Almost never: *How are you doing?* or *Whassup?*

We are shown to an English-style bar whose ancient jazz ensemble is a local institution.
Sweet Lorraine swings by the neck at the end of a plausible rope, a pendulous weight lags
behind the beat. There's an uncomfortable tension in the harmony, hoping gravity will
release the tune.

Auld Lang Syne & rumor of misdemeanor . . . *think you might forge a bill of lading
for a few dollars more . . . ?*

                                                they are all hard of hearing,
                                                because they are very old—

given a pork *baozi*
with chrysanthemum tea
            —and their badness is loud.

        Graeme, the Melbourne wine importer, has seen mobs at the train station in
Beijing, "Unless you can act Chinese, pushing and shoving *en masse*, you don't even
think about it."
        His newly arrived sommelier agrees, "There is never any queuing and officially
you can't use the people's money . . ." he adds, chewing an antacid.

•

The Peace Hotel in Shanghai still makes a big deal of Noel Coward's visit in 1930.
It was here, then known as the Cathay Hotel, that he completed *Private Lives* while
recovering from flu, moving about his suite in silken noetic outbursts inspired by
gin and tonics.

In the dining room, coffee spoons are lined up regimentally on linen, waiting to be selected
by the approach of a hand from within the simultaneity of their reflective bellies.

The terrine holds a catarrh chasing broth. A shimmering hake creams in a chafing dish.

Sunlit metrics
                incline through drapes, quadrilateral prisms fall on a carpet of trapezoidals.
The devil's in this house,
& in my prose.

Here is a strange place to put a Rabbi.

In a corner of Diaspora searching the lost tribe of Asher,
                                                in Hongkew, he tells it.

He gave me a ride to the district so I could show him. In a hired black sedan with the
curtained windows of a hearse
                        we try to find the location of a kosher restaurant in old
photographs,
a family of Russian exiles during the war.

His uneasy return to an enterprise is mentioned, a chemical process in
                                                textile manufacturing.

Return in a joint-venture corporation is spoken of. We compare similarities in facades, we
visit eyeglass shops & lavatories that are the functioning ends of sewers.

Here is a half-moon bridge grandma might have wanted her name said on, who dreamed a China of the imagination.

Mandarin allusions in her attic scrapbook had memorialized a Currier & Ives Oriental of this place,

Shanghai in the 30s, a glut in sentimental paintings of cerulean landscapes, nocturnes with yew trees.

•

Mine was a life planned to go wrong.
There is no reasoning with me about this.

In my case money might be of great service to me but probably it would not. If I do not convert my opportunities there is no need to have my opportunities increased.

We look over the bridge and see our own effigies floating in the water
framed by the arch below.
                            Dragon-patterned koi drift into the exhibiting
umbrage of our outlines beneath a surface of sun-fired clouds.

How can that depth be known where we see ourselves reflected?

I have acquired a knowledge of the grades of Suzhou tea, and of temple steles in provincial towns,
                        but have no authority or expertise
                                                for time spent with a Cantonese chrestomathy.

That's China dirt! I said,
                    stamping my boots like a kid in a sandbox.

We should never need to ask, racket in hand, "Tennis, anyone?"

•

The business of leisure has brokered a misty theme package to Nanjing.

It is sometimes necessary to distinguish likeness from likeness. A particular human being is being contained and brought in for scrutiny, detained close to the metropolitan stands, or the picaresque rogue. The viewer sees what portraiture has revealed.

City of sirens
I enter the city of declamation and anonymity
                              from the calcined glare of New Jersey,
entered by slipping under the rock in Weehawken.
Nobody here but us chickens!
                    In New York the Metropolitan's interior has a kind of
creamy emollience resonant of marble lavatories. There is a serial structure of supreme beauty accessible to the unconscious—a collection of artifacts has become a single ready-made.

If there is such a fiduciary accounting, make mine a scrapheap.

There is some oblique knowledge
discovered when you've retained the distinction between home-baked and homemade pies from a teen mother who worked at Maid-Rite.
                              There is a difference, when given a
chance to make the distinction, but the memory is not of that distinction. It is domestic, maternal,
            a thief at the window.

& that is a greater mystery
that enigma is cumulative
in forgery and forgiveness
in a slice of pie.

In desultory shopping
nothing in particular lacks me.

I've made garlands of flowers
& nothing but the cords that bind them
are my own.

(if we're lucky)
we speak a protean grammar

"Take it easy and enjoy! [*Suiyi!*] You must stop hoping for a life of promise,"
he concludes, using the long curved nail on his little finger
to clean the nails of the others.

I cannot account for a damaging willful naivety—which once lost left me with the sense
of failure that I didn't have what it takes to be disguised to myself successfully.

•

"Name *things*, instead!" Nutmeg, Tianjin Free Trade Zone, a great wall, the seas, restore them intact, as notions to the mind.

Let me tell you of a peasant named Wu.

                         Over and again he had done what was the thing required for initiation, without going on to redeem himself—so that he faced the ridicule of the amateur, dilettante, or just plain failure of the quitter. It looked to some of his neighbors as though Wu's ambitions were low and easily satisfied with a disgraceful solemnity; as if he were a feeble minded victim of his own worship for another's skills, and found delight in servitude. In reality he refused occupation after occupation, but continued to make his public profession.

There is nothing more irritating or more stupid looking than the sluggish spectator who turns up on stage by mistake. He must perform or clear out; the world has no use at all for the clumsy.

MENU

Three kinds of twilight
Seven kinds of fried
The clitellum of an earthworm
Cross-section slabs of Jurassic ammonite with plum sauce
Portion of merlon on crenellated wall
14 numbered circumlocutions
A coign morticed corner Hunan style
Lassitude with wet noodle

"Americans," he tells me in confidence, "are known to be adventurous."
No one can believe all the pigeons in New York, "We would have eaten them!"

To lose occupation but continue to make profession
is slow death. ☺
19   20   44   58   23   88

•

Fei Xu was a hoarder. He had not lived an authentic life. At every turn he did not choose to go into that life, the road that would authenticate the singular struggle to have chosen and remained what he might be, while being there, in a place he already was.

His floors sagged with newspapers and printed ephemera. It burned one night and consumed him.

"Perhaps," the Master answers,

"you are too hard on yourself."

"But I am neither small nor mean enough for that," Grasshopper replies.

•

The streets I remember were etiolated and birdless.
There were no rhapsodic eventualities.

The dark is deeper within.
                              It is personal.
This is where we are stunted
like light starved houseplants
blanched apparitions in the Orient night.

Though I didn't know it at the time,
This is the quality of a self-darkened place.

The hole is deeper than China.

•

At Yu Garden the smell of scallions perfumes the square,
In a crowd
        photographers with chrysanthemums
beneath the Longhua Pagoda, "What do they call you boy?"
asks a big Western confidence man
                            in the same tone of voice
a man uses when he gives a Hopi kid fifty bucks to throw his goat
into the Grand Canyon
               instead of posing next to it for five.

We have every Moon Cake filling and festival food, but are uncertain whether our
concerns of government are shallow. We are too curious to be understood.

If, on the other hand, her activities expressed the government's ignorance of world
opinion, she could easily expect prison.

•

At the state dinner for foreign advisors
I arrived with Xiao Yan. Her mini skirt
causing a fuss that had to be explained
to Public Security—she isn't unescorted.

There is talk of Foreign Service Officers
and what befell them. The China Hands
[*Zhongguotong*] who put signs in the park,
NO DOGS OR CHINESE.

We are aware these taipan with their mandarin lives
are considered our big-nosed kin, though our hosts
are too polite to say we are ancestral.

We are fond of the crab canapés and shrimp satay.
We've noticed that Magnolia Brand cigarettes
are mild and flavorful.

We speak, each in our noisy pool of murmur,
"She said, she thought that was very perceptive of you!"

In his boast they are learning the courses of a $600 meal.

An overseas Chinese
named Lu
            came back to Shanghai
fifty-years after his father fled, as Nationalists
were driven out of the city. He is the affable owner of an American Bar.

In the thirties this establishment had been a brothel on the fringes of the International Settlement, an extraterritorial zone where Chinese and foreigners came together [*huayang zachu*] in mixed company. In spite of the years, and the karaoke, it still had the amber feel of the era, with hard wood paneling, the smell of linseed oil, red-shaded cocktail lamps. Used after Liberation as a butcher's counter, the bar was stained and pitted by cleavers. Lu poured *shaojiu* [firewater] to the English, and Remy VSOP to Chinese. It was one of the few places for conversation with noise reducing booths and a 30-watt atmosphere—a place for romancing phantom opium, in hopes of finding the place still in pre-liberation brawl. Lu understood this, and even cultivated an air of criminality, to offset an actual criminal element.

ON NATIONAL DAY EVE

We mingle with the Minister of Petroleum.

We are addressed by the Mayor of Shanghai.
A cadre of deputies welcomes us, Zhu Rongji
bids us "soft landing"
        with a toast,
           "Dare to make decisions in the cultural exchange."
           "*Ganbei!*"

           "Gaige Kaifang"
           [Reform Opening]

           He cannot mean it—& he does, all the same.

These few preservations
at the very edge of retention,

        that bulge in his pants, is the rootless orb of lotus
           in a multitude of cant associations.

The cheongsam fits the Chinese figure well
but they say it looks like a cheap suit on a Western female.

      In the ginkgo trees on Fuxing Road a line of wash
          was whipping.
              Unsolved,

a piece of monkey business with her scarf
as she passed on her bicycle.

      There is a service being sung in the grotto beneath the truncated
         spires of St. Ignatius, with what obscenities
            lopped off by Red Guards.

To see in the sun-struck diocese
the molesting charity.

•

What BLUE is to America
                              RED is to China
A favorite color,
a field for stars.

Between word and recognition a citizen must be willing to die for something believed
without too much conscience. The most difficult circumstance is without doctrine.

   Color that is surrogate for heaven's pastoral of infinite blossom.

•

With what cold original voice comes an aboriginal silence in the giant bamboo.

I listen

in a wilderness, for a human memory of one billion

looking anxiously for something that, while it is expected, and seems to be present, has gone.

The way out was the way in.

I turn east to feel the rain,

& hear the water song in the dripping grove.

I walk on New Year's Day by a road of China local.

The path leads to a scenic view behind the temple.

Coals raked over space.

Revenant stranger,

in an enormous night.

●

        "You are heavy-lidded," she said to me. "You have almost epicanthic folds."

In the large censorious room our mutual admiration was facetious. I thought at first this was some deficiency in me, and would not listen to the small voice that carped.

In written Chinese it is impossible to forget that personality once meant, not the soul, but the soul's mask.
                  Each suspected
it was our own ingeniousness that led us to admire so much
                      the other's gifts.

•

Why would they not appreciate the ceiling with her? There must be a word for
whelmed—
                    to appreciate something the exact amount, rather than step on someone's
            momentary and private
observation of something's ardor.
There's something obviously dishonest about putting it all together. And still, we look up
and see what she means, all at once,
                    though none of us exactly know
        what we are looking for
in the celestial motif.

I wish I could appreciate what the world has done to you
but just now I am throwing rocks at tanks.

—A disciple

OCCUPATION OF A RED PAGODA

I smoke Hongtashan cigarettes. They cost me 12 yuan a pack,
half a day's wage for the worker who sells them to me.

Here are the words: 红塔山
Shan, the most pictographic, is Acme,
ubiquitous shining mountain,
symbol of quality.
Hong, means red. I know this
because I used to smoke Hongmei,
after the flower of a red plum.

Allegedly, workers bribe officials, though imported brands are more desirable to the
cadres. I am told a carton of Hongtashan makes a good gift, though not as good as a
carton of "555" or Marlboro. This is China long ago now, when it had 300 million
smokers, according to the Ministry of Health, "making cigarette production a profitable
enterprise for foreign investment."

For those around me, smoking a premium brand was like breathing money.

•

It was out in the country somewhere, a border town. She worked for an organization that taught girls to speak enough English to ask their Johns to use condoms. There was a lineup of quail-eyed girls, sitting around on couches and chairs. Do you like me? A couple of them asked. But most were inchoate and shy.

My friend was disappointed in me for not choosing one of them. She said I had hurt the girls' feelings. At her statement I became, later, sick in mind. Not because of divided principles, but because her precociousness offended a cleaner instinct. It would have been better if I had not followed her through the door—through which there were no exits. Years later I would even have the opportunity to regret. Now, as it stands, I am the only one left who remembers this. That singular, delayed regret was inspired by a different woman, one I was involved with much later, who made me feel I had wasted the privilege of being a man.

When I went back on assignment I was changed. I did not lose my focus as easily, I had a clearly prescribed task and my curiosity was rewarded with stories of people more interesting than me. I was able to remain aloof, detached though observant, and completely unlike myself in an earlier period of, is it, the word that now comes to mind, *deliquescence* with the world? There was a decision to be made, and I made it without thinking there was a choice.

Very soon, I'll begin freediving for abalone off Catalina with a friend who had access to a boat and sold our catch to a Korean wholesaler. I'll carry on a one-sided conversation with John for years, never able to determine what I did to him.

EVENING OF THE FIRST MORNING

How to say
bagatelle
a dear but useless
attention to things
satisfied
as they are

What portion
can we have
who awakened
from a common dream
no language
plain enough
to say what the real
is made of

Let out late
to meaning
in hesitation
at the rail
before evening
and black water
collide

In the Quarter
slant-light striking
one corner of
a darkened cross
one intersection
at the end of Dauphine Street
lit with blaze

And (here) I will go back for the poems of John Clare's madness, which I should have
bought but are not there when I return for them. Why is it I do not buy things; what is
wrong with me?

I lost a chance to take that domesticated

                                          temperate nature into mine

elm into a redwood forest

        tree that made a mordant lamplight on my bedroom walls, that murmured

                  in our chimney *thou owned a language by which hearts are stirred*

Deeper than by a feeling clothed in word, And speakest now what's known of every tongue,

Language of pity and the force of wrong.

why this   mine
rejection of the elaborate
English by the
machinist's son—
I break these
lines   willingly—individual
of no significance

•

What have I to do with the city in which I sleep? Toward which I am beginning to feel faintly inimical. Fumblingly I examine the responses I receive, the correspondence of a friend with whom I once had a brief personal contact.

A being comes into a city with certain attitudes and is inculcated with others of his time. Then one day the light has an elevated shift, ten years have passed, everything is reordered; a decade, and already an anachronism, prognosticator of another time. In New York, a city that despises strivers, in a country which views anonymity as an injustice, there is a certain foolishness in propriety, documentary paternity, declarative wisdom for what the city is.

•

In the years I was there the economy of Shanghai grew 19%.
It was like living on a theater set

constructed day and night.

I won't forget the ludicrous sound of steam-powered pile drivers as we made love,
banging mechanically to a hollow thud in the bedrock beyond the wall of the institution,
conscious & too aware
        of our involuntary
        syncopation,
                trying not to laugh
                        at the Chaplin industrial
                        of rhythmic concupiscence

      —her brutality and her courage

she knew what she wanted though she no longer knew how to ask for it

      —there was his obsession with the husbandry of emotional resources

he knew what she wanted when he understood what she didn't mean

      —reached,
           between a distinctive but intangible quality and being
                they
ideal and actual . . .

           a portion between   not
           the portion that is written

here should be the description of one who wished he'd had the security to be less
selective but choosing too soon, and the fear of pregnancy, and being stuck in that shit-
hole for the rest of his life.

•

I became extraneous. A man unable to say I—correctly—to my
satisfaction. It is better when I did not know
there was an I to be delivered, to a casual & unsympathetic
over-thinker. I think of Rell Sunn, the surfer—
resting, as she lived, at Makaha. I will not forget her,
that there was a child in the surf. Out there, & what is to be
resisted— . The body resisting in water
the tendency to be absorbed, letting go her energy on a wave's
energy. Where are all the children I once knew? And I don't
mean them that were there when I was, but them that
knew me as Uncle. Where is the mirror of apprentice?

I know many children to whom I would fain make a present on some one of their
birthdays, but they are so far gone in the luxury of presents—have such perfect museums
of costly ones—that it would absorb my entire earnings for a year to buy them something
which would not be beneath their notice. *Journal,* Nov. 5, 1855

•

Because America
  the Louisiana Purchase made Old St. Jo, Missouri State; subset Platte
  Purchase; Buchanan County; Midland Empire; hell-broth of Mulligans
  crossing to Oregon, or death in a sod plastered room.
Because America,
    it is worth noting
the grand-nephew of Martin Van Buren, a suit and tie man, a haberdasher like Harry
Truman, lived near Dr. Williams in Rutherford, New Jersey.

Because America Joe Brainard 8 Greene Street 10013
     gave up his public memory to read Victorian novels. Because
  America
Abe Vigoda.
   Because America: Louis Agassiz & John the Revelator, and withered apple
dolls in cornhusk skirts; because Madame Chiang Kai-shek and Billy Wilder and Betsy from
Pike. Because America as I watched Buster Keaton in his last years I hoped that he would
not be the Buster Keaton we knew, that he would be a friend of mine.
   Because America Henry Thoreau was your personal adjutant and you don't
even show it—having for many years been self-appointed inspector of invisible public good
that was in jeopardy
    & he did it faithfully,
      without receiving a cent of our tax dollars.

Because America who can say what America is; 75-odd thousand efforts a day, held together
  by the love of a very few people. In combination the cheapest and angriest
  people ever made by God, though paradoxically generous to victims of natural
  disaster and giving of gift wheat.
Because America your fatalistic drum of low prices. Because Jesus Loves You America.
  This I know, your beautiful–hot–gorgeous–forgetful–Jesus Loves Me.
Because $64 in my pocket today. America, I could probably give you more.

•

I remember those first parties we attended in Shanghai. I had the agonizing feeling on arrival of being utterly out of place. I had known dens of privileged association before, but those were of like-minded people, associations into which I fit easily because of their demotic nature (free congregations of easy beings), but whose overly cultivated sensibilities nonetheless, like my own pretensions, affected me negatively. It was difficult for me to remain among the like-minded for very long. I need enemies. Here, with the United Nations, the sons and daughters of diplomats, scarified princes of African countries, and the flotsam of the mercantile exchange, I was unknown and impecunious, a poet in a rich Bohemia, a society where easy money, the confident gesture, and the displays of quick and questionable success were all in evidence. I had a sneaking feeling that I was invited there because Carolina was attractive, and I felt like a sort of pimp, or peg-legged corsair with an exotic bird on his shoulder. Before these celebrity's children of the bank and bar who were the shining lights of these affairs, I was something less than nothing—a life unconsidered, they could not conceive of such an unattractive fate. No one but Carolina paid the slightest attention to my beliefs. Though they might listen curiously if I tried to talk, their attention would be off with the slightest entertainment. I had the options of sitting in a corner and listening, or facing someone and pretending to listen. Once or twice in desperation I tried to get in on the extended conversation, but even with the help of liquor I fell flat against the flamboyant sentimentality of the lawyers and the extravagant lyricism of the sons of bitch exporters. There was always a conflict within me between what I knew myself to be and what vanity prompted me to be, and I was as a consequence subject to nervous spells of pettiness which I mistook for earnest belief. In the end this conflict would unsettle me completely.

I believed I was living a persona. I now realized Glenn was the persona, for a self in reserve. I was its life. It was a being whose particular characteristics I could not remember to recreate exactly on a daily basis.

TOLSTOIANA

His brother's attitude to the country made him uncomfortable and irritated him. To Joe the country was the background of life—that is to say, the place where he rejoiced in receivership of the world, suffered, labored; but to Tom it meant on the one hand rest and leisure from work, and on the other an antidote to the corrupting influences of the city, freed him from its illusions and opened his mind to accept the great world beyond.

To Joe the country was good because in it he knew what his labor meant at the end of the day—the usefulness of which there could be no doubt. To Tom the country was good because there one could and should, unless by choosing, do nothing. And when Tom's attitudes toward country people grated on his brother's nerve, Tom would tell him how he *knew* country people, and he could talk with them—which he did well, without apparent affectation—without them feeling condescended to, and Tom would deduce general conclusions in favor of the simple life and its people and in confirmation of his fair treatment and superior knowing of them.

Joe could not accept this kind of attitude towards his neighbors. He regarded his neighbors chiefly as participants in a common drama, and while he could be an enthusiast for their strengths, and rougher characteristics, when their actions called for other qualities, exasperated with one or another of them for his carelessness in starting a fire, drunkenness, lying, or just plain and stupid filth.

Had he been asked whether he liked his neighbors, Joe wouldn't have known what to answer. He was ambivalent about them, and it would have shown. Being a good-hearted person he liked people, generally, and in a subdued way. But like or dislike the people he had come from, whose characteristics he had imbibed with his mother's milk, as something apart he could not, not only because he lived among them and all his interests were bound up with theirs in a social contract, but also because he regarded himself as part of these people and did not see any special qualities or failings distinguishing himself from them. He could not contrast himself with them. He had no definite views concerning them, and would have been at a loss to answer the question whether he knew how he and his neighbors appeared to the rest of humanity. For him to say that he knew his neighbors would have been the same as to say he knew the world.

•

In Shanghai the new architecture was parvenu and all too willing to materialize the Flash Gordon fantasies of the West—viewed from the Bund the Pudong district across the river had become the imagined East of Ming the Merciless.

What I resented about the new money in Shanghai was their presumption to global taste, their cultural fluidity, and their inability to understand my privilege was not like theirs, but one of my making. They did not value my privilege to reject them, their hard won but ersatz cosmopolitanism. They had no antennae for a cultivated regionalism from the original province of their ambitions. They could not understand that my failure was not preordained, but intentioned.

•

For myself, I didn't want to end up as one who had spent their lives pursuing minutiae, a hoarder, least of all a collector of my lucky personal discoveries. But people I admired had done just that. American Silas Marners, socially penurious, who smelled of tannin and butter, their teeth coffee stained, hair matted and oily, their scent musk, fingers smeared with Elmer's glue, copying source material and templates from bra catalogues and photo magazines into scrapbooks, discovered in trunks, spare rooms, or beneath their death beds. America was once full of smelly amateurs

: and experts of indelible topics,
                                        tramping through the weeds to pastured cairns of obscure
                    individuals.

& yet, everywhere, professionals deny they have professions.

Free
            as given, without wanting.   Not an improvisation.
The last available act of defiance in American life
COMPETENCE
                            : the amateur dedication, of a mendicant
                        artisan

                the least thing done well
                            something preposterous—and homemade.

•

Unknown persons were the most exciting to me, those who died without confessing. Especially when it became known that I would also die unknown—that I had what it takes to be forgotten in a day like any other. I considered myself nothing more than a fact, and felt others might be nothing more than things unto themselves—named & identified, but unbelieved, strange—as when an experience is complete, absolute, & there is euphoria of pure phenomenon, & blue despair of an interrupting personality.

I had the advantage that I found within me all that was needed to hate what I did. Most of all I wanted clarity. I had to realize that it was already always and I was never going to be more specific to myself.

The most practically important question had always been how I would get my living. The perfection in doing was to do nothing
out of the ordinary.

It is the paradox of fragments that they are the workshop of conclusions, and of such conclusions as have rarely become the basis of conviction.

•

There is the belief
that I am stepping into a river of eternity.

There is the belief that led to an infinite labor.

They work for very little who understand and appreciate time. For them
time does not count, suspended for years in the presence of their desire;

to cultivate doubt—so that work perpetually resumed & recast, gradually,
has the secret importance of an exercise in self-reform.

There is a gradual move away from that which is finished, a finished thing of mind,
to a power of transformation always in action, in flux,

in spirit, a matter not of meaning or conveyance,
except in time's obliterating duration.

•

there is
in the thought
I live

the dead end
of significance

PRONOUNS

How thoroughly we enjoyed that. How we went home and laughed ourselves unhinged until we were holding our stomachs and Emily had to come down and tell us to shut up before we woke the baby. For most of these creatures you can be as the ghost dancer, walk invisibly across their path while you steal their souls. They invite our self-abnegation; they think it is about them, that you care more for them than you do for yourself. You flatter them with nothing more than your attention, and they believe it is because of who they appear to be. But they are seemingly unknown to themselves, when all the while you're watching their soul slip down the hem of their outfit and pool at their feet. You're thinking of the hollow thing left there talking to you, and how impossible it is that a thing such as this, which was made up to be an intelligent creature, has no antennae for the superior consciousness clearly in observation of it all. And so you tell them exactly who you are, without the explanation they did not seek. The only power you have, *being*, is more powerful. There's a self-satisfaction with the communal ground at a party, the connective coagulate. There must be something wrong with him who hasn't managed to engage them, or manages too directly to engage in recognition, what is taken for candor. They don't understand how you can know so much about what they do, and they know nothing of you, but the unembellished fact of having arrived before them, which they cannot perceive as true. They ask about your profession, which they believe like a hometown or a choice of overcoat, will give the basic pattern of your character. They are in awe of trades. They deny, constantly, though they trade on what they do, that they profess an occupation. And with no *society* they are immobilized by its honest observations of them. Which is not sincere. You withhold from them your soul's mask but in withholding how can they know if you defy them?

It never occurs to ask, "What do you *do*?" "How do I *know* you?"

•

And when we are in the life we wanted

who wonders we are there

where they would not go.

Sometimes, in conversation, I would turn and notice a single brick in the opposite wall, or stare at the nose in front of me and hear its voice. Remarkable how long we can believe an inwardness that merely ails ourselves. Not to say I want to be left alone.

We are the desperate party to ourselves, which hold each other in captivation.

To be peregrine in these excoriated thoughts is to be a stranger. Are you not also available to it? The greatest ignorance does not disgust like knowing.

Who are aware of us as we are of them?

APOSTROPHE

There were business lunches of exquisitely prepared food that would give no more joy than a bowl of cold oatmeal, or satisfaction in the knowledge that it was even nourishing.

And the meal cost me nothing—being expensed—so left me with a sensation of the empty prandial transaction I had just put inside my guts.

After some business dealings with men, I am occasionally chagrined, and feel as if I had done some wrong, and it is hard to forget the ugly circumstances. I see that such intercourse long continued would make one thoroughly prosaic, hard, and coarse. But the longest intercourse with Nature, though in her rudest moods, does not thus harden and make coarse. A hard, insensible man whom we liken to a rock is indeed much harder than a rock. From hard, coarse, insensible men with whom I have no sympathy, I go commune with the rocks, whose hearts are comparatively soft. *Journal,* Nov. 15, 1853

ENTHUSIASM

Midway through my journey in life I became moribund with the corruption of self-improvement, impoverished in a suffocating mesh of conceits—studious—moralizing—contrite—a man unable to say *I* correctly to my own satisfaction, annoyed to be recognized for what I became, which I myself wished to become.

It was better when I did not know there was an *I*.   *to be* believed.

Of these tendencies, the tendency that offended me most was the moral element, whose surrogate for rage was indignation and repentance.   *to be* sickened.

HOMAGE TO HAVANA

Let's strip the deck for action
                              now we have our hours in China
—let us remember to half-comprehend what we must deem to be
        or doom our interpretation to infinite regress.

And over noodles at the night market the Doctor said, "Once we have an awareness of it,
it's hard not to become intensely fascinated by what it is, what it might be, what portion
of a satisfying inwardness I ought to have."

Let us remember the PhDs and my thoughts, my humble, fond remembrances of the great
baccalaureates. . . . The wind that night, the clamor of incessant shutters, doors, and Huang
tiptoeing the successive patios trundling with typical smoke in hand on his way back from
the head—and the misty acumen of the mystic yeomen,
                                        superb and enduring
the poets of rivers and mountains
of parochial unity
        who opposed the cosmopolitan stands in woods to lope and pronk
allegedly lapsed into unknown mastery
                        with the terrible apartness of flies.

NIGHT WITH A TRAMP AND OTHER NIGHTS

I lie about in the open fields at night, knowing I can go home, that I can give a good account of myself if I need to, if I am harassed by the police I can prove I have a home.

I can say instead that I am conducting a kind of experiment in free living. If my life allows a free form of vagrancy. From home I can conduct my homeless business.

I will say this is my house, my wife is here, and soon a child. You can see what I am.

Why haven't we heard of you? presumes that we should have been heard of.

•

in your house there was once
a first spider in the clean wood

but how far can we trust the sinuous rill

are we in fact
sentimental enough
for the anti-sentimentalists

REGULUS

Near the window—within a momentary sphere of comfort—reference to torture
perpetrated by the Carthaginians: It seems they took this poor bastard out and cut
his eyelids off. Then they kept him in a dark hole for a while. When he was fully
acclimated to the dark they brought him out in the midst of the day, and turned
his face full against the sun. His torturers repeated this until he was blind, before
disemboweling him. When I read this, lying on a velvet chaise in a borrowed house,
I recall a Schubert CD was on the deck, I thought of the elaborate apparatus it took
for him to compose that music. I thought the lattice of indulgences available to him.
To make music like that is to be only vaguely aware of the rest.

●

—summer over
gave back
the house—

last grains in the hour
glass widening whirlpool
in an emptying tub—

sliver left of a soap
—economy
of anything that is ending—
both hurried & prolonged—a late
exit—things quickened
by use—toward the ended

narration—
with patrician diction

—he left my mother
she'd done him wrong
but he stuck inside her

half-nasty—
a success

when her mother told her
to abort—

didn't

—make his experience
illegitimate
did not tell me
he broke her jaw

AT SAN MICHELE

Life has not yet returned a dream. My thoughts on the vaporetto, amid the jewels of Venetian architecture: penuriousness had prevented me from an actual life. Imagine hiding out years in waiting that what had been might come & that to live without expenses or consequence could be done.

And now, to have no need of money, or equivocation & endless management over so many negligible transactions—to, for instance, want something & deliberate until you were nauseous & had wasted hours in the street, not knowing whether or what it might cost you—what its true cost was—down the line.

Now, within certain limits, to want for nothing; though little is changed by this. My economy needed only money
                                    : to prove itself.

If I had only bought the coat when I needed it, I might have worn it to the next one. Instead, I held it in wait, which cost me nothing, and went unworn within me.

I have prayed when it counted, and denied it when expedience required omission.

I have been made to regret nearly every selfless act I was capable of. But only after it became clear I had flung myself into an ingenious activity. Those I willingly desired to work for conceived the sacred notion that they were my benefactors, in bestowing upon me so much pleasure in their entertainment. And when one day the job was done & my resources were exhausted by it—my benefactors, my peers, had been paralyzed by my alms.

•

It is good once again
to have a room
          without a view of books.

      . . . another's mind. &
     what good is left

our sacred places
           given back
as once there was a grove of neglect
turned new
       by our forgetting.

Positano

•

He asked me to name one thing that I love.

I love the crickets' public sound.

Who have sent their crafts toward our longing.

•

I would meet with some provoking strangeness

                                         or is it that I am to be merged
to disappear into these manners,
in satisfaction and success

dodging in the most shameful way my fullness of meaning.

•

We are as things named & recognized but wonder at what has become of us.
There is only so much reading of the underground to be done.

The making of a sentence is a way of remaking the mind
in hesitancy & occupancy   in residence   FULL

& this spirit, that lyrics have not synthesized, is a stranger's life
by all accounts
                    —though it is nothing before the words can be found.

To believe nothing is to believe in believing
independent of a beginning thought.

There is life after language.

In the dead end of significance, an awakening object,
a thing loved for itself.

The awareness scenery
                    of others and ourselves.

Founded on the faith of a verb
                    to be
                                    in genesis and separation.
We are as we do not know.

A tactical Orient
                    who were not captive.

The word into which is written the name.

•

When a dog runs at you, whistle for him.
He will think he knows you.

Hearing an old set of retouched
affections, in his bafflement.

NOTES

liumang	Gangster
拆 *chai*	To be destroyed; dismantle; pull down; slated for demolition
是 *shi*	The verb *to be*; yes
新 *xin*	New; to renovate; to make new
p. 40	John Clare, "The Fallen Elm"
p. 43, 54	Henry David Thoreau, *Journal*

Glenn Mott was born in St. Joseph, Missouri, educated in its public schools and at his grandparent's tavern. He studied at the University of Missouri, the University of Alabama, and graduated to the People's Republic of China. In the early 1990s he lived in Shanghai, teaching at East China University of Science and Technology, traveling widely in China and Southeast Asia, returning later as a journalist. His poems, essays, and translations have appeared in journals and newspapers in the United States and abroad, including *L'Anello*, *Poetiche*, *The Bund*, *The Missouri Review*, and *Fulcrum*. He lives in Brooklyn, New York.